BECOMING AN EVANGELISTIC CHURCH

It's Really Not that Complicated

CHUCK LAWLESS
with the Church Answers Team

Becoming an Evangelistic Church:
It's Really Not that Complicated

© 2026 by Chuck Lawless
© 2026 by Church Answers

All rights reserved.

ISBN 979-8-9883649-9-3

Church Answers
Franklin, Tennessee

Printed in the United States of America

Unless otherwise indicated, all Scripture quotations are taken from the *Holy Bible*, New Living Translation, copyright © 1996, 2004, 2015 by Tyndale House Foundation. Used by permission of Tyndale House Publishers, Carol Stream, Illinois, 60188. All rights reserved.

CONTENTS

INTRODUCTION 5
Chapter 1: Yes, Your Church Can Be Evangelistic 9
Chapter 2: Evangelism and the Enemy 19
Chapter 3: What Research Says about the Harvest
   Fields 29
Chapter 4: The Powerful Principle of Intentionality .. 39
Chapter 5: Know Your Community, Reach Your
   Community 49
Chapter 6: Praying Evangelistically 59
Chapter 7: Why Preaching is So Important 69
Chapter 8: The Evangelistic Small Group 79
Chapter 9: Our Great Omission: Why Evangelistic
   Churches are Evangelistic 89
Chapter 10: A Discipleship Pathway that Leads to
   Evangelism 99
CONCLUSION 109

INTRODUCTION

I was a PhD student at Southern Seminary in Louisville, Kentucky, and Thom Rainer was the dean of the Billy Graham School of Missions, Evangelism and Church Growth. When Thom invited me to join a research project for a book that he was writing, I jumped at the chance.

That 1995 research project looked at 576 growing Southern Baptist churches to determine what made them evangelistic. Part of my responsibility was to tabulate the results of a survey we sent to these churches. Believe it or not, I tabulated the results by recording answers on graph paper in those days. The work was tedious at times, but the book resulting from the study, <u>*Effective Evangelistic Churches*</u>, quickly caught the attention of pastors and other church leaders.

What most intrigued me about that study was the focus: we studied only churches that were seeing growth through reaching non-believers. The churches we studied at the time were churches that met these criteria, in Thom's words:

> We somewhat arbitrarily decided to examine only those churches whose annual baptismal total exceeded twenty-five for that year. We then determined that a church must have a baptismal ratio

(resident members/baptisms) of less than 20:1. In other words, the church was reaching at least one person for Christ for every twenty members.[1]

We have adjusted the criteria over the years in defining an "effective evangelistic church," but the principle remains the same: we want to make sure we're studying churches that are growing by conversion growth rather than by transfer growth. That is to say, we study growing churches who are reaching non-believers rather than only swapping sheep with other churches.

And, that's the insight I gained from Thom so many years ago: *church growth studies must focus on studying churches that are actually reaching non-believers.* These churches live on the front edge of "make disciples" (Matt 28:19) even as they typically also have intentional discipleship plans to keep those they reach. It's simply not enough to study growing churches without asking the source of their growth.

What might surprise you, though, is *how* that insight I gained almost thirty years ago has affected my life since then.

As a follower of Jesus, I continually evaluate my own evangelistic efforts. I want to be doing evangelism naturally, but I work hard to make sure I'm building relationships with non-believers, living the gospel in front of them, and speaking the gospel to them.

As a senior professor of evangelism and missions (which basically means I'm an old prof), I want my

students to ask, "If the church I lead is growing, are we growing by reaching non-believers or by transferring in new members?" To not ask the question is to risk getting comfortable with transfer growth.

As an elder in a local church, I want my church to ask the same question. All of us need to make this question a personal one. To be Great Commission congregations, we must ask if we're making new disciples through evangelism, baptizing them, and teaching them.

This passion for evangelism that drove Thom years ago still marks him—and consequently, it marks our Church Answers team as well. You will hear my voice throughout this book, but it's really the collective work of our entire Church Answers team because we share the same passion for evangelism as we carry out our respective responsibilities. Our prayer is that we might help you gain that passion, too, if you don't yet have it. We are praying that this resource will help move you in that direction.

CHAPTER 1
Yes, Your Church Can Be Evangelistic

You know from the introduction that I've known Thom Rainer a long time—more than 30 years, actually. He's an entrepreneur who dreams big dreams and an evangelist who loves the gospel, a combination which makes him a leader among the leaders at Church Answers. He genuinely longs for the day when believers and churches are doing evangelism in such a way that all we can say is, "God did that."

A strong leader, Thom is. A technological wizard, though, even he would agree he is not.

That's why I'm not that surprised by his story about a thermostat problem at his home that Thom described as, "The thermostat works just fine, but no one could seem to figure out all the buttons and controls. Even the service person asked me if I had a manual that explained all the controls and options." He didn't have a manual, and looking online or using AI seemed a bit silly. All he wanted was a thermostat he could understand.

So, now he has a new thermostat—one with an off/on button, a run/auto button for the fan, a heat and air conditioning switch, and a place to set the temperature. The new thermostat is really not that complicated. It's basic.

Well, you might be wondering what place a story about a thermostat has in a book about evangelistic churches. If so, here it is: this book is about simplicity. It's about the basics. It's about grasping the fact that evangelism in your church is not rocket science. It's actually more important than rocket science. It's eternally important.

But it's not that complicated.

How Did We Get Here?

Our team at Church Answers have researched, written, and created resources for evangelism. We have led over 1,000 church consultations. We have coached thousands of pastors and church leaders. There's always more to know, but we've learned a lot about local congregations. And, though evangelism is the work of the Holy Spirit, we understand how some churches are reaching people with the gospel, and why most churches are not.

It's really not that complicated. Just where are we, based on our studies?

- Our team does most of our work in North America, particularly in the United States and Canada. American churches as a whole are evangelistically anemic.
- Though defining the evangelistic effectiveness of churches can be subjective, we try to bring a level of objectivity to the task by calculating a "conversion ratio." The ratio simply shows how many

people are reached for Christ relative to the average attendance. For example, if a church had 12 conversions in a year and an average attendance of 100, its conversion ratio would be 12 percent (number of conversions divided by average attendance). We can say with sad certainty that the conversion ratio is steadily declining in America.

How, then, did we get here? The following statement is a tautology—that is, it states the obvious through redundancy—but the essence of the story is this:

Churches stopped being evangelistic because they stop evangelizing.

We realize that statement seems obvious, but we want to make a point. Churches that are evangelistic have pastors, staff, and church members who are evangelistic. Churches that are not evangelistic have stopped trying to reach people for Christ. It's that simple.

What Did Jesus Say about Evangelism?

Jesus commanded us to reach people for Christ through Great Commission passages in the New Testament like Matthew 28:18-19: "I have been given all authority in heaven and on earth. Therefore, go and make disciples of all nations, baptizing them in the name of the Father and the Son and the Holy Spirit."

Another well-known Great Commission verse reflects Jesus' words right before He ascended to heaven: "But you will receive power when the Holy Spirit comes upon you. And you will be My witnesses, telling people about me everywhere – in Jerusalem, throughout Judea, in Samaria, and to the ends of the earth" (Acts 1:8).

A verse that perhaps does not get as much attention is Luke 10:2: "The harvest is great, but the workers are few. So pray to the Lord who is in charge of the harvest, ask Him to send more workers into His fields." According to the words of Christ Himself, the harvest really is great; there are lost people still to reach.

The problem, Jesus says, is not a barren field—it's a lack of workers. It's reluctant Christians.

That's why our Lord asks us in this text to pray for obedient workers. The lost people in our communities are waiting on us.

Evangelism through the Local Church

Evangelism can and should take place wherever the opportunity presents itself, but God designed the local church to be the hub of evangelism. God gave us the local church as His plan A for ministry on earth, and He did not give us a plan B. If local churches are healthy, they will be doing evangelism. When evangelism is not a priority, local churches are not healthy.

Such is the reason we are passionate about the local church and evangelism at Church Answers. What's important to Christ is important to us. We want to see more churches telling the good news of Jesus to a dying world.

On the other hand, please hear us clearly: God *is* at work in many churches in America. He can also be at work in your church.

One of those churches is in the Nashville area. The congregation is about nine years old. It was birthed with a vision and passion for prayer and evangelism. It's in a large metropolitan area, and it's in the mythical "Bible belt"—but neither fact is the reason for its evangelizing people. Nor is it because they've discovered an evangelistic formula unknown to other congregations.

To the contrary, the church is evangelistic for a very basic reason: the leaders and many of the members are evangelistic. Again, it's not rocket science.

It does, though, raise the question: "Why are the leaders and members of this church evangelistic while evangelism is not taking place in most churches?" We will cover these following areas throughout this book, but here are four key reasons.

Reason #1: The church members tell each other about their salvation.

Do you want to jump start the evangelistic culture of your church? Ask the participants in your small groups to share the story of their salvation with each other and the group. We know of one leader of a small group who asked some group members to tell their story when she called on them, and their stories inspired and motivated others in the group to tell their stories.

Think about how important it is that we tell our stories to one another. It's simple—we're not likely to tell our stories to non-believers if we don't even tell our stories to other believers. We won't take a risk to tell a non-believing world if we don't tell our stories where it's safe.

In that same church, all baptismal candidates record their salvation stories on video. The entire congregation hears how they became Christians and learn about specific people who were key influencers in their story. These baptismal stories are powerful reminders of how God uses typical Christians to share their faith or invite someone to church.

Reason #2: The church members tell their stories to people outside the church.

After a season of encouraging members to tell their stories to each other, the pastor and other leaders encouraged the members to do the same with those outside the church. The pastor mentioned in sermons and announcements that the members should pray for opportunities to tell their stories to non-Christians. The process was not high-pressure, nor was it guilt-laden—but it was effective.

The breakthrough took place when two members told the pastor they had shared their salvation story with people outside the church. He asked a student at the church to videorecord these members telling their stories in no more than three minutes. The church then showed each of those videos to the congregation in consecutive weeks.

The church culture began to move outwardly. More members shared their faith and stories. Hardly a week went by without the congregation hearing yet another story of faithful obedience to the Great Commission.

The video of one church member summed it well: "I told my story to my hair stylist. Because I knew her, and because I prayed for the opportunity, sharing my faith was both natural and supernatural."

Reason #3: The church ties prayer to evangelism.

The church member was on target when she said, "because I prayed for the opportunity, sharing my faith was both natural and supernatural." Though God uses us as conduits for the gospel message, the power is from God and God alone. Our responsibility is to pray, go, and tell in that power.

We know of thousands of churches who have seen God use the Church Answers resource *The Hope Initiative* in their church—a resource intentionally built on prayer. Through a 30-day guide, each participant focuses on the power of prayer. The desired outcome is for the church to develop a culture of evangelism, but the program is powerless without the power of prayer.

The resource is a simple strategy anyone can do. Anyone can participate. Anyone can develop an evangelistic heart. More specifically, anyone can pray. Anyone can be a tool for God to use. The program's not built on complexity; it's built on simple obedience.

Pray. Go. Tell. That's basic intentionality. These churches have decided to pray and evangelize again. They started being evangelistic because they started evangelizing.

Reason #4: The church intentionally plans evangelistic emphases.

For certain, it's a start to talk about evangelism and encourage church members to be evangelistic. Ultimately, though, evangelism must be action-oriented. The Great Commission of Matthew 28:19 does not say "think about it," or "encourage others to do it," or "study it"; it says "Go" and "make disciples." Evangelism must be an action.

When we consult with churches, we often look at the church calendar to see where the church's priorities are. If we see one evangelistic emphasis on the calendar each year, we've learned that we can be fairly confident the church is holding its own. If we see two evangelistic emphases, the church is likely reaching people. If we see three or four evangelistic emphases in a calendar year, though, we know that the church is likely to be in the top five or ten percent of healthy churches.

Evangelism is an action—and you can do it. Your church can do it.

It's simple obedience. Pray. Go. Tell.

It's not rocket science.

It's simple, actually.

The title of this chapter is not incidental. Your church *can* be evangelistic.

Let's begin the journey through each of the next chapters to see how it can happen in your church.

It's time to be obedient.

It's time to pray, go, and tell.

CHAPTER 2
Evangelism and the Enemy

We've seen it happen far too many times.

A church begins an evangelistic focus, and the members start to catch fire for telling the good news of Jesus. Though their efforts are slow at first, they pick up steam as the members start telling their gospel story to their family members, their neighbors, and their co-workers. The pastor's heart beats with anticipation.

And then the devil hits.

Sin happens. Internal church strife arises. False teaching worms its way into a small group. Denominational issues distract the church leaders. All the extra "stuff" quenches the evangelistic fire. The devil and his forces always fight against believers and churches who start telling the gospel story.

Why Does the Attack Happen?

There's a reason that attack takes place. The Bible is clear about the state of non-believers, and that description often reflects language of spiritual warfare. Take a look at the italicized words in these verses:

- "Once you were *dead* because of your disobedience and your many sins. You used to live in sin,

just like the rest of the world, *obeying the devil—the commander of the powers in the unseen world. He is the spirit at work in the hearts of those who refuse to obey God.*" (Ephesians 2:1-2)
- "If the Good News we preach is hidden behind a veil, it is hidden only from people who are perishing. *Satan, who is the god of this world, has blinded the minds of those who don't believe.* They are unable to see the glorious light of the Good News." (2 Corinthians 4:3-4)
- "For he has rescued us from *the kingdom of darkness* and transferred us into the Kingdom of his dear Son, who purchased our freedom and forgave our sins." (Colossians 1:13-14)
- "Then they will come to their senses and escape *from the devil's trap.* For they have *been held captive by him to do whatever he wants.*" (2 Timothy 2:26)
- "And I will rescue you [Paul} from both your own people and the Gentiles. Yes, I am sending you to the Gentiles to open their eyes, so they may turn *from darkness* to light and *from the power of Satan* to God. Then they will receive forgiveness for their sins and be given a place among God's people, who are set apart by faith in me." (Acts 26:17-18)

Because that's the condition of people we need to reach with the gospel, it shouldn't surprise us that the enemy comes roaring against us with vengeance if we start doing evangelism. He and his forces really do go about like lions, seeking believers they might devour (1 Pet 5:8).

How might he attack your church? We doubt his strategies have changed much since the Garden of Eden, so let's consider them.

Attack #1: False teaching

Just as the serpent denied the veracity of God's Word when he told Eve, "No, you will not die" (Gen 3:5) after God had told Adam otherwise (Gen 2:16-17), the enemy seeks to refute God's Word today. Think about some of his strategies with us, and consider the effects the enemy's teachings would have on evangelism:

- He wants us to believe and teach there are multiple ways to God, despite verses like these:

"Jesus told him, 'I am the way, the truth, and the life. No one can come to the Father except through me.'" (John 14:6)

"There is salvation in no one else! God has given no other name under heaven by which we must be saved." (Acts 4:12)

- He pushes the idea that good people go to heaven apart from a personal relationship with Jesus, in spite of these kinds of teachings:

"No one does good, not a single one." (Romans 3:12)

> *"For everyone has sinned; we all fall short of God's glorious standard."* (Romans 3:23)

- He wants us to believe that some people are so bad they are beyond the love of God, thus ignoring biblical teachings like:

> *"When you were slaves to sin, you were free from the obligation to do right. And what was the result? You are now ashamed of the things you used to do, things that end in eternal doom. But now you are free from the power of sin and have become slaves of God. Now you do those things that lead to holiness and result in eternal life."* (Romans 6:21-22)

> *"You used to live in sin, just like the rest of the world, obeying the devil—the commander of the powers in the unseen world. . . . But God is so rich in mercy, and he loved us so much, that even though we were dead because of our sins, he gave us life when he raised Christ from the dead. (It is only by God's grace that you have been saved!)"* (Ephesians 2:2-5)

To be fair, our Church Answers team has seldom seen this kind of aberrant theology in evangelistic churches we've studied—and there's a reason for that fact: it's a biblical theology of the lostness of human beings and the significance of the death of Jesus that compels churches to be evangelistic in the first place. Where a church is genuinely committed to reaching non-believers by calling them to turn from their sin and trust Jesus, you will generally find a strong biblical theology.

So, this recognition of the enemy's strategy of false teaching is as much a warning as it is a research finding. Your church won't do evangelism if you believe there are many routes to God, good people go to heaven, and bad people have no hope anyway. The enemy wins (at least temporarily) any time a church takes such a position.

Attack #2: Sin

We're all responsible for our choices, but we can't deny the enemy's role in dangling bait in front of us to draw us into disobedience. In cooperation with a world that also pushes against God, Satan desires that we cross the line into sin and then attempt to hide it just like Adam and Eve did. He knows that when we're hiding in our sin, we're not likely to be in the streets telling people about the good news of Jesus.

Ongoing disobedience and passionate evangelism hardly go hand-in-hand.

I'm afraid we at Church Answers have seen this problem lived out. Over the years we have been studying churches, we've seen leaders of strongly evangelistic churches collapse morally and wound their congregations in the process. Evangelism then becomes even more difficult when non-believers in the community question the integrity of Christian leaders and doubt the power of the gospel in the first place.

We want you to know, church leader, that you have a bullseye on your back if you want your church to be evangelistic. You're a target. Your ministry's a target. Your home's a target.

Let that thought sink in a bit . . . and we'll come back to it later in this chapter.

Attack #3: Division

This strategy, too, is not new. In Genesis 2, Eve was God's special gift to Adam – a helper God created just for the first man. In Genesis 3, though, everything changed when sin entered the story and Adam then blamed Eve (and ultimately God) for the problem. The intrusion of a serpent into the garden led to division in the first home, including not only husband against wife in Genesis 3 but also brother against brother in Genesis 4.

The enemy's arrows of division were effective then. They've been effective between then and now. And, they're still effective today, as evidenced by the deepening divisions that mark so many churches in North America even as I write these words. No church embroiled in internal controversy and conflict will be intentionally and effectively evangelistic at the same time.

False teaching.

Sin.

Division.

All tools of the enemy to keep your church from evangelizing your neighbors and the nations.

Where is your congregation most vulnerable as you move toward becoming an evangelistic church? What steps will you take to guard against Satan's arrows as you engage the darkness?

What Do We do about the Battle?

There's a reason we've included this chapter as the second chapter in this book. The first chapter laid out the purpose and direction of this book about evangelism—a topic that invites the enemy's attack on me as the writer, on our Church Answers team as the supporting cast, and on you as the reader.

Our team knows from experience that the enemy will urge you to give up any thought of your church becoming evangelistic, close this book now, and not read another word.

We're pleading with you to keep reading if that's the voice you're hearing. Too much is at stake when we're talking about God's people telling God's story to a world desperately in need of God's good news.

So, read on – there's hope!

The Bible is clear that the war we're in has already been won.

The serpent God judged in the garden (Gen 3:14-15) is the adversary Jesus disarmed by His death on the cross (Col 2:13-15) and the devil He will cast into the lake of fire in the end (Rev 20:10). Satan has been bound, he is being bound, and he will be bound. We're on the winning side!

Church leader, the enemy wants you to ignore or deny the teachings of the Word of God regarding lostness and salvation. Instead, stand hard on the Word. Don't let a loser deceive you.

He will call you toward the sin line and invite you to live in the dark spaces of hiddenness and defeat. Don't go there. Get another believer to walk with you, fight the battles by your side, and push forward with obedience. In the words of a friend of mine, "Just don't do stupid!"

The enemy will also promote division in your relationships and your congregation. Prepare for, and counter, his attacks by strengthening your relationships. Love your spouse fully. Model godliness before your children. Say, "I'm sorry" to church members and ask forgiveness when needed. Love even non-believers with godly love. Don't give the enemy a foothold toward division.

A Starting Point

In light of all we've said in this chapter, we want you to hear an important caveat. Our Church Answers team has seen the enemy gain the upper hand in far too many churches, but we've also occasionally seen *individuals* in broken, divided churches still widely telling the story of Jesus. God often works through those few believers to transform lives of non-believers—and even an enemy-rocked church will at least take note of something unusual happening.

Seeing the hand of God change lives simply has a way of showing us the foolishness of listening to the voice of

EVANGELISM AND THE ENEMY

the enemy. In that sense, effective evangelism is both a target for the enemy *and* a weapon against the enemy's arrows.

So, how should you stand against Satan when he attacks your church for being evangelistic? Just keep evangelizing!

It's really quite simple. It takes only one . . . or two . . . or three to get started.

Your church becoming an evangelistic church can start with *you* becoming an evangelistic Christian.

Satan and his demons won't like it—but that's okay. They're already defeated anyway.

CHAPTER 3
What Research Says about the Harvest Fields

Sam Rainer, our Church Answers president, tells this story. Many years ago, his wife him called to inform him she had bought a bushel of corn. Recently married, they were new to the Indiana community where Sam had started serving his first full-time church. Having grown up mainly in the city, he had little knowledge of harvesting procedures or standardized weights and measures of crops. His wife, being a country girl, knew precisely what she was doing.

"Do you want to help me shuck the corn when I get home?" she asked Sam.

"Sure, glad to," Sam said. He wasn't exactly sure what the verb "shuck" meant, but he played along.

Then, he took one look at the back seat of his wife's vehicle and realized his challenge. A bushel of corn weighs 56 pounds, and he wasn't sure there was any way he and his wife could consume that much! He just hadn't given much thought to what a good harvest of corn that year would require of him.

Let me apply that story to the church. Remember Luke 10:2? Jesus told us that the harvest is ripe, but we don't have enough laborers. We focused more on the laborer shortage in the first chapter, but this chapter is more about the harvest opportunity.

In Sam's research, too many churches in the North American mission field don't have a "harvest" mindset. Instead, they only compete with other churches over existing believers while assuming that those on the outside want nothing to do with Christianity. Let's look at what the research says about that assumption.

The Hope for the Church—including Smaller Ones

Here's what we know. Over the last 50 years, church growth has largely been "transfer growth" as people shifted from one congregation to the next, typically from smaller churches to larger churches. The median church size in 2000 was 137 weekly attendees, but the median church size today is 65 weekly attendees. Though there are exceptions, larger churches have generally grown at the expense of smaller churches.

However, this movement from smaller to larger churches is beginning to wane, partly because there are fewer people to pull from smaller churches anymore. The sixty or so attenders who remain are usually older (the typical church member is over sixty years old) and are not likely to transfer to another, larger church. While it is true that the largest churches are continuing to get larger, there are fewer and fewer larger churches.

The number of these large churches increased

exponentially in the 1980s and 1990s, but around 2010, this exponential growth stalled. The megachurch movement reached an inflection point with about 1,600 megachurches in the United States. Over the next ten years, up to the pandemic of 2020, the number of megachurches dropped to about 1,200. The pandemic then caused many megachurches to drop below 2,000 in average weekly attendance. There will always be healthy megachurches across the nation, but it's likely the phenomenon of megachurch growth is no longer rising. Some other model must now take the lead.

Smaller and midsize established churches have an opportunity for growth in a healthy way *if they start intentionally doing evangelism again.*

Even churches in decline can experience revitalization *if they go back to the basics.*

The harvest is still abundant if you pray, go, and tell.

How the Unchurched Really Feel about the American Church

Our team at Church Answers recently conducted a research project that took several months to complete. We wanted to know if unchurched people feel differently about the church than those who are regular attendees. We found new, surprising insights from the unchurched.

Most of the unchurched are not unfamiliar with churches.

One of the first surprises from our study was that "unchurched" does not mean unfamiliar with the church. Over 60% of the unchurched individuals surveyed said they attended church regularly as children. These aren't strangers to Sunday mornings; they're former attendees. This reality reminds us that evangelism today is often more about reconnecting people to Jesus than about introducing them to something entirely new.

We are clearly becoming a less churched nation. However, the reality of childhood memories of church among the unchurched gives us hope. We can pray that God will use those memories, relationships, and former rhythms of life to reawaken the unchurched. Evangelism sometimes begins not just at the edge of belief, but also at the edges of memories.

The church still matters to the community.

Despite the prevailing narrative that the church is losing relevance, our research shows the opposite: both churched and unchurched individuals believe churches are generally good for their communities. In fact, nearly 6 out of 10 unchurched respondents affirmed this position. The unchurched aren't hostile; they're cautious, indifferent, or disconnected, but they still believe the church can be a force for good.

This perception gives churches an open door. While people in the community may struggle to connect personally with local congregations, the unchurched generally have a favorable opinion of the concept of church. The opportunity lies in turning that abstract goodwill into concrete, local trust. Reaching that goal will take work, though, as the next finding shows.

Local trust in churches is often missing.

Here's where the challenge becomes clear. While people admire the idea of church, they often don't trust actual churches in their communities. Only 38% of the unchurched said they viewed local churches favorably. And, the trust gap widens further when it comes to church leaders: just 35% trust pastors. Conversely, regular attendees generally trust their churches (81%) and pastors (76%).

On the other hand, the unchurched view the church as more relevant today than churchgoers do. While 40% of churchgoers said the church is largely irrelevant, only 27% of the unchurched felt the same. Their problem isn't perceived relevance; their problem is trust.

The dichotomy is fascinating:

- Churched people: "I trust the church, but I'm not sure it's relevant today."
- Unchurched people: "The church is still relevant, but it's not trustworthy."

Why the disconnect? Two factors stand out: insularity and scandal.

On one hand, less than 1% of churches prioritize evangelism as the church has become largely inward-focused, relying more on transfer growth than conversion growth. "Harvest" for them is grabbing somebody's else's crops rather than sowing seed, watering it, and celebrating when God produces new life.

On the other hand, high-profile scandals have also shaped public perception about the church. Unchurched people may like the idea of church, but they're not sure they can trust the people inside the church near them. Yet, hope remains. . . .

Friendship becomes the bridge to reach the unchurched.

More than half of the unchurched believe the church could be a great place to make new friends. In fact, 8 out of 10 unchurched people say they would attend a church service if a friend invites them and goes with them.

However, nearly 60% also say churches feel intimidating when they're visiting. That intimidation, paired with a lack of personal invitations, keeps the unchurched away.

Church leaders, take note: the greatest evangelistic tool we have is not a new program or worship style. It's friendship. It's relationship. That single insight should revolutionize how we train and equip our people.

To the unchurched, confusion over church is a greater barrier than high standards or rules.

Our study shattered another common myth: the idea that unchurched people avoid church because of rigid rules, moral standards, or high expectations. In reality, only 4 out of 10 unchurched respondents said churches have too many rules. But, over 60% of the unchurched—and just as many churchgoers—said churches are confusing for outsiders.

People aren't repelled by theology or rules. They're puzzled by church processes. They don't understand what we're doing or why we do it. I still remember my own confusion when I went to church for the first time as a non-believer, and that was more than five decades ago!

The solution? Clarity. The more open and understandable we and our processes are, the more likely people are to engage. For example, a clear membership class that explains the church's beliefs, structure, and expectations up front is essential for healthy church growth.

The unchurched aren't sure church is a good place for family.

Because of the confusion and lack of trust, many unchurched people don't believe the church is a good place to raise a family. While regular attendees overwhelmingly believe the church is a good place to raise families (85%), the unchurched do not share the same perception. Only 44% of the unchurched agree or strongly agree that the church is a good place to raise families.

These numbers should concern us, but they also offer a call to action. What if your church became known as the safest place in town for families? What if it were the go-to space for helping families grow? This opportunity is ripe for the taking.

Among the unchurched, indifference toward the church is more common than antagonism.

So, then, why aren't the unchurched coming to church? It's not because they're mad, too busy, or hostile. It's because they're indifferent. The most common reasons they gave were: 1) they don't see church as necessary, and 2) they simply got out of the habit.

This reality is both sobering and empowering. If the main obstacle is apathy, then the answer is intentionality. The solution isn't to defend the church against attackers—it's to lovingly engage those who have drifted or those who've never engaged the church in the first place.

God's Work and Our Obedience

When asked what would prompt them to start attending church again, the unchurched pointed to two things: a spiritual reason (a desire to grow spiritually or a prompting from God) and/or a personal reason (an invitation from a friend or spouse). These answers affirm a powerful truth: evangelism is both divine and relational.

God must work.

And, we must be obedient.

We cannot manufacture the Spirit's prompting, but we can create environments where invitations flourish. Every church member has the ability to say, "Come with me. I'll sit with you."

Many church leaders obsess over worship style, programs, and branding, but the research shows that the unchurched care less about these things than churchgoers do. The top reason people—both churched and unchurched—attend a church is because someone invited them. While style and programming can enhance the experience, they are not the driving force behind new engagement. Personal relationships are.

Finally, what kind of church do the unchurched prefer? Unchurched people lean slightly toward non-denominational congregations, but Baptist, Catholic, and Christian churches also rank high. The key insight isn't the label; rather, churches that are easy to understand, relationally warm, and spiritually authentic will have the most impact, regardless of denominational affiliation.

The Challenge

The harvest fields are not empty. They are ripe.

The unchurched are not angry. They're available. They are not uninterested in faith. They're simply waiting for clarity, trust, and a friend to walk with them.

Church leader, the time to act is now. It's not that complicated—somebody outside your church's walls is waiting.

Let's become evangelistic churches, because the harvest fields are more ready than we might have thought.

Of course, Jesus already told us this truth.

CHAPTER 4
The Powerful Principle of Intentionality

Thomas Edison was the ultimate inventor/entrepreneur.

He combined relentless curiosity with practical innovation and business savvy. With over 1,000 patents in his name, Edison revolutionized modern life through inventions like the phonograph, the incandescent light bulb, and the motion picture camera.

But he didn't stop at inventing. He built entire industries around his ideas. He founded General Electric, which was one of the most influential companies in the world for decades (in fact, GE was one of the major employers in the city where my second pastorate was located).

Edison also pioneered the concept of research and development labs. When he pursued a new idea, he did so with passion, excitement, and expectation. He felt like he could change the world with his ideas.

And indeed, he did.

Our Discovery

We have a passion at Church Answers: to discover what God is doing in evangelistic churches. This passion began with Thom's zeal and has captured the rest of us. And, if we learn of a principle or activity that other churches can replicate, we want the world to know about it.

We had our own Edison-like excitement when we began seeing patterns in evangelistic churches. We've seen sufficient numbers now to believe that the pattern is both meaningful and applicable. Again, the finding wasn't rocket science, but it was nonetheless amazing . . . and simple.

If a church has at least one evangelistic emphasis on its calendar in a year, it will be more evangelistic than 80 percent of churches in North America. Of course, we know our numbers are not precise because we evaluate churches where we consult, coach, and converse. The sample size and selection do not meet strict statistical criteria. But, we have observed these churches long enough to feel confident that we are directionally accurate.

Still, there's more.

If a church has at least two evangelistic emphases a year, the church will be more evangelistic than 90 percent of churches. With three evangelistic emphases a year, the church is in the top five percent. Add a fourth emphasis, and it's in the top one percent of churches in North America in terms of evangelism.

Did you get that? At the risk of redundancy, hear again our tautological statement from the first chapter of this book: *evangelistic churches are evangelistic because they decide to do evangelism.*

THE POWERFUL PRINCIPLE OF INTENTIONALITY

It's all about intentionality.

So, where does a church leader begin? Again, the answers seem almost too simple.

Get It on the Calendar

Pam and I have been married for 34 years. If I want to show her that she's priority in my life, I know what I need to do: schedule dates, trips, and other activities on our calendars. I have to go beyond conversations to action—and that takes planning.

Do you want your congregation to become an evangelistic church? Get evangelistic emphases on your calendar. The possibilities are many:

- Plan an *Invite Your One* Sunday every year (www.inviteyourone.com).
- Make *The Hope Initiative* a part of your church's regular rhythm (www.thehopeinitiative.com).
- Add a sport from Upward Sports to reach your community (www.upwardsports.org).
- Take gifts to neighbors in your community using the Good News Neighbor Toolkit (https://bit.ly/4itTNrg).

We recently heard through Upward Sports about a church that offered pickleball to the community. If your church were to do something similar, you could add *The Hope Initiative* twice on the calendar since it's a simple, 30-day program. Then, add *The Good News Neighbor Toolkit* (usually done within two or three hours) twice a year, and your church would have five evangelistic emphases per year.

Again, it's all about intentionality. And again, it's not that complex or difficult.

Use Stories to Stir Action

Another of our member churches at Church Answers intentionally shows a three-minute video once a month in their worship services. Sometimes the video is of a person to be baptized that Sunday, as we described in a previous chapter. One young lady told her story about how she became a follower of Christ after her husband left her. It was a powerful story of redemption and hope.

Think what might happen when your church regularly hears stories of redemption. Not only will they know each other better, but they'll also be more excited about what God is doing in your church. They'll want to go and tell others.

They'll want to talk about Jesus.

What might happen, too, if you get permission to post those testimony recordings on your church's website under a tab like, "Stories of God's Grace at _____ Church"? Maybe a hurting member of your community will find hope in Jesus.

Stories inspire. Stories motivate. Stories honor God.

But, getting and telling stories must be intentional.

Start today, perhaps with your church's small groups telling their testimonies within their group.

As a Leader, Model Evangelism

Several of us on the Church Answers team have been pastors. Some of us still serve in that role. All of us both recognize and wrestle with this reality: evangelistic churches are typically led by evangelistic pastors. In fact, I'll go so far to say that I've *never* seen an evangelistic church without an evangelistic pastor. Never.

We wrestle with that truth because we know it puts the onus on us to lead the way. Yet, it's a reality. When the pastor is evangelistic, the church is evangelistic. When the pastor is not evangelistic, the church is not evangelistic. Leaders who model and do evangelism are key to effective church evangelism.

Years ago, I listened to a pastor/student complain about his non-evangelistic church in a Doctor of Ministry seminar Thom and I were leading. When the student finished expressing his concern, Thom asked him one simple question that penetrated every one of us in the room: "When's the last time you shared your faith with someone?"

I suppose you know what happened. The student looked at his feet and painfully admitted his own failure to lead the way. Thom challenged him to share the gospel at least once a week for the next six months and keep him informed along the way. Again, you can probably figure out what happened.

Everything changed. A Great Commission-disobedient pastor became an obedient one, and his church followed in his footsteps. By the way, that renewed pastor also did what we encourage pastors to do: he told his church what he was doing. In sermons, in newsletters, in casual conversations, he talked about sharing Christ wherever he could. He let his joy overflow into modeling evangelism for his church.

He was being intentional.

Build Evangelistic Awareness into Sunday Services

The worship service is an opportune time to create an evangelistic culture. Our Church Answers team worked with a pastor in Arkansas who told us that he wants every service to have an evangelistic emphasis, including challenging the members to be evangelistic.

Based on his interaction with the church and his watching a portion of one of the services, here's what Thom learned. Each service has a dedicated ministry/prayer time of about five minutes. Members pray on their own, and some gather in groups together. The prayer time is preceded by a "ministry moment," a quick video where a member speaks about what God is doing in his or her life.

A church member gave a quick story about how she invited a friend from work to go to church *with her*. Those last two words, "with her," are important. The members at this church understand that an invitation must mean that the church member goes into the church building with the guest. In fact, the pastor humorously and rhetorically asked, "How many of you have been invited to dinner where the host is not expected to show up?" An invitation to church is not really an invitation unless you go with someone there.

The most moving part of the video was when the church member described how her co-worker came to church, saw the radically different lives of other Christians, and heard the gospel preached. The member said, "She didn't stand a chance!" Everyone laughed.

Then, she concluded her video with, "This friend is still my friend. More than that, she is now my sister in Christ. I would like you to meet her." At that very moment, the two ladies surprisingly came on the platform as the congregation applauded thunderously. There did not seem to be a dry eye in the worship service. Thom, too, cried as he watched the video.

Pray with Evangelistic Intentionality

I may not eat three full meals a day, but I do eat something at least three times a day—which means I also pray a blessing over food at least three times daily. That's usually without much effort, too, since that's what we're supposed to do.

I have to work at praying evangelistically, though.

We'll talk about prayer more in a later chapter, but I trust you get my point now. The ongoing work of prayer can take effort, but any church that has sustained evangelistic fruit is a praying church. More specifically, it is a church that is praying for lost people.

Praying for them by name.

Praying for God to save them.

Praying for opportunities to share the gospel with them.

Praying for more laborers to join the church members in the harvest field.

That kind of heartfelt praying doesn't happen by accident, however. It happens because believers like two of my pastoral heroes intentionally set aside time daily to intercede for non-believers.

They pray, and they evangelize. . . . and then they pray more.

They know you can't separate the two.

Be Consistent with Evangelism

Evangelistic churches understand something many others miss: consistency in outreach matters more than intensity. A big outreach event once or twice a year might create some excitement, but it rarely builds lasting momentum. Evangelism thrives where simple, intentional steps happen on an ongoing basis, not just when a big event is on the calendar.

We created *The Hope Initiative* to offer churches something simple, doable, and potentially consistent. From our early versions of *The Hope Initiative* until today, evangelistic church leaders understand that they must keep the mandate and privilege of evangelism before the church members.

After all, it's easy to let evangelism die out unless you intentionally and continually keep it in front of people.

In these churches, leaders regularly challenge people to pray for the lost by name. They encourage members to invite someone almost every week, not just at Easter or Christmas. Evangelism training is not just a one-time workshop; it's built into the DNA of the church.

This kind of steady faithfulness builds a different mindset. Evangelism becomes both supernatural and routine—supernatural because God works through it, and routine because the church lives it on an ongoing basis. Their consistency not only keeps evangelism before the congregation, but it also keeps them motivated when results are slow.

Always Think Intentionality

In the end, great evangelistic churches aren't chasing emotional highs. They're building a culture where evangelism happens naturally, week after week. Simple, steady steps have a powerful impact over time.

That, simply stated, is the powerful principle of intentionality.

CHAPTER 5
Know Your Community, Reach Your Community

Your address isn't an accident. God, in His sovereignty, has placed you exactly where you live. Whether you value your neighborhood or just tolerate it, God has a purpose for you: to love your neighbors and reflect Christ to them.

Even the unique ones. And, we all have them at times.

Sam and his wife, Erin, had a neighbor they watched daily as he was, in Sam's words, "in his backyard, robed and barefoot, gathering sticks from the neighborhood and performing what could only be described as a kind of interpretive dance around a small fire."

Pam and I had a country neighbor who, when one of the turtles from our pond wandered into his yard, shot it and fixed his family some turtle soup. We had another neighbor who had statues of pigs in his front yard.

Even when our neighbors are harder to love, a healthy spiritual life means a heart for the people right outside our front door. God's mission sends us to the nations, but it also sends us across the street. For some, getting on a plane is a bold move. For others, it's stepping across the lawn and saying hello to a neighbor.

Everyone everywhere needs the gospel, including those right around you.

Your home, your job, your school—they're not accidents. God has placed you exactly where He wants you right now. Your neighbors are not random. They're part of God's plan. They might, in fact, be someone that you, your family, or a member of your church family leads to the Lord.

Find Out Who's in Your Community

Let me tell you two personal stories to help you think about this responsibility. The first story relates to the second church I pastored in Ohio. I had been pastoring there for almost a decade when I had an opportunity to do a substitute teaching stint for a ninth-grade English teacher who had to step away for a quarter of the school year. During that quarter, I learned more about my community by talking to school administrators, fellow teachers, and freshman students than I had learned in all my efforts as a pastor the decade prior.

Frankly, I hadn't been talking to enough people about the community I said I wanted to reach. I hadn't been doing my homework well.

Years later, I served as a volunteer firefighter in another state where I was then serving as a seminary professor. Again, I had been in that city for over a decade when my firefighting responsibilities took me to parts of the community I had never seen. I had lived in that community for years—but in only one part of it. I was ignorant of the ethnic and economic differences within a short driving distance of where I lived. It took riding through the city on a firetruck to realize I was trying to be a gospel witness in a city I really didn't know very well.

Churches sometimes do the same thing. They want to make a dent in the darkness around them, but they haven't done much study about the darkness. They often wrongly assume that their congregation reflects their community, simply because they're never done any genuine study of their community.

That's one reason our Church Answers team created the "Know Your Community" report (https://churchanswers.com/solutions/tools/kyc/know-your-community/). Churches will pray with more focus and strategize with more intentionality when they really know who lives around them. Knowing their community is critical to their reaching their community.

What I've learned, though, is that churches often don't know their community.

When I lead a church to do the "Know Your Community" report (or any other demographic report), I ask to see the results before the church's leaders do. I review them, and then I quiz the church's leaders about their understanding of the community demographics before they see the actual results. I can't remember the last time I've worked with a church who accurately knew their community's demographics. Even churches who truly are seeking to reach people are often trying to reach a community they don't really know.

That's a problem... especially when it's simple to get the demographic data of the community.

Love the People Right Next Door

God's mission moves forward through one primary vehicle: the church. Just as many different types of cars share the road, a variety of churches—each with their own style and personality—carry the good news of Jesus. No single congregation owns the kingdom, and every Bible-believing church can be a powerful force for God's mission.

In your neighborhood, people will typically view your church in one of three ways:

1. Negatively – They know who you are and wish you weren't there.
2. Neutrally – They don't know you or don't have an opinion either way.
3. Positively – They know who you are and are glad you're part of the community.

Unfortunately, some churches stand out for the wrong reasons. Sam reports once seeing an invite card that said, "We're probably not the church for you!"—followed by a list of things the church was against (which makes you wonder if the church understood what an "invite" card should be). The message came through loud and clear, but not in a way that pointed anyone to Jesus.

More often, however, churches are simply unknown. People drive by the building daily without knowing anything about the congregation inside. In our research and consulting work across North America, this "neutral zone" is where most churches find themselves. When we interview local residents about churches, we often hear the same phrases again and again even when the church is sometimes literally across the street:

> "I've never heard of that church."
> "I didn't know that was a church."
> "I have no idea what they do."
> "Where did you say that church is?"

Our goal should be to move our churches from being negatively known or unknown to positively known. We do that by loving our neighbors well, gaining their trust, and shifting the neighborhood's perspective.

How do we best do that? Again, the strategies we suggest aren't that complicated.

Invite neighbors to worship—and to lunch.
Imagine if even ten percent of your congregation made it a regular habit to invite neighbors to worship and then shared a meal with them after church, either at home or in a local restaurant. This simple act communicates hospitality, care, and a desire for genuine connection. Sharing a meal also has a way of disarming people and creating space for spiritual conversations.

Your neighbors may not remember every point in the sermon, but they will remember how your people made them feel welcomed over lunch.

Sponsor and coach local sports teams.

Some churches sponsor youth sports teams, especially when a church member is the coach. Doing so is more than a financial contribution—it's a relational investment. Practices and games become opportunities for gospel influence. Coaches can pray with players, show integrity, and build relationships with parents. Over time, these connections often open doors for conversations about life, faith, and church.

Join neighborhood civic organizations.

Most communities have local service clubs and nonprofits doing good work. We can build trust when church members and leaders show up not to control the agenda but to serve the organization. Be present, consistent, and helpful over time, and people begin to associate your church with care and concern for the community's well-being.

Hold meaningful Christmas Eve services.

Christmas Eve is the one night each year when many unchurched folks are open to attending church. They may be nostalgic, lonely, or seeking hope, so don't treat your Christmas Eve service like a checkbox on the calendar. Plan it intentionally. Preach clearly. Make guests feel expected and welcomed. A well-executed Christmas Eve service can be a spark that ignites someone's spiritual journey.

Minister to first responders.

I've already told you I was a volunteer firefighter years ago. I honestly hadn't thought about it enough before then, but first responders put their lives on the line every day—and many of them have given little thought to their spiritual condition. They face life and death situations, but often without considering eternity. Find out if the first responders in your community have a chaplain, and work with that chaplain to determine ways you can serve them. You might find that the simplest expressions of gratitude open a door to individual conversations about spiritual matters.

Support foster families.

Foster families often feel overwhelmed and isolated. Churches can step in with meals, supplies, prayer, and emotional support. If even one family in your church fosters, dozens of people in the community—caseworkers, biological parents, teachers—might welcome your church's compassion. Foster care is hard and holy work, and supporting it makes your church an advocate for the vulnerable. It might also open the door to evangelism.

Open your facility to the community.

Too many church buildings sit empty five or six days a week. Why not use your space to bless others? Some churches partner with Christian preschools, host meetings and events for local nonprofits, provide space for a polling center, or open their Family Life Center doors for an "open gym" weekly. Your church can become an integral part of your community, and these various partnerships can lead to gospel conversations and deeper trust.

Begin a prayer-walking ministry.

There's something powerful about walking your neighborhood, praying over homes, schools, and streets. Prayer-walking helps your congregation develop spiritual sensitivity and local awareness. As members walk and pray, they'll begin to see people not as strangers, but as neighbors God loves. And, when people in the community discover your church prays for them, they might reframe how they see your presence.

Do something.

Every church has the potential to make a lasting difference in its neighborhood not by being the biggest or flashiest organization, but by being faithful, present, and loving. The goal isn't to impress the community, but to serve it in the name of Jesus. When your community begins to know your church for its hospitality, generosity, and compassion, people will take notice. Somebody will pay more attention to who your church is.

So, start where you are. Use what you have. Trust that God will use your church to shine a light right where He has placed you. *Just do something.*

Pastor, Love Your Community . . . and Stick Around

If you're a pastor, permit me a minute to talk with you directly. The most evangelistic pastors I know are those who see themselves not only as the pastor of a local church, but also as a pastor of a community. They love where they live. They're invested where they are. Unless God clearly leads otherwise, they've planted their feet solidly on their current ground.

See, it's tough to lead your church to be evangelistic in your community when your eyes are always on the supposedly greener grass in a different location. And, frankly, it's hard to love a community you're continually seeking to leave.

So, pastor, love your community. Pray for them. Get to know them. Seek to reach them through evangelism, and challenge and equip your church to join you in the task. Stay awhile, and watch God work.

Don't overcomplicate the work—just do it!

CHAPTER 6
Praying Evangelistically

I often tell the story of how I first heard the gospel. It wasn't a preacher who first told me about Jesus. It wasn't a traveling evangelist. It wasn't a Sunday school teacher or small group leader.

No, it was seventh-grade classmate. A 12-year old.

He loved me enough to want me to know about Jesus, so he told me the gospel story every day of my entire seventh-grade year. I had little interest in being a Christian, but I listened out of kindness—all the while looking forward to summer break when I wouldn't have to deal with my friend again.

Well, I made it to summer as a non-believer. I was sure the battle was over at that point since I wouldn't see my friend for several months—but I was wrong. Very wrong.

I was wrong because my friend cranked up his praying for me when he couldn't talk directly with me each day. He did talk to someone every day, but that someone wasn't I.

My friend talked to God every day about me. About my soul. About his burden for me. About his pleading with God to save me. About his hope that my Christian conversion would occur sooner than later.

I didn't know it at the time, but my turning to Jesus as my Savior and Lord in August 1974 was surely the result of the prayers of my friend and his mother and grandmother. All of them prayed regularly for me, and God drew me to Himself when I was 13 years old. The combination of the proclamation of the Word and the prayers of God's people made an eternal difference for me.

Why We Need to Pray

It's really quite simple. As we've said throughout this book, this stuff is not rocket science. We must pray because none of us has the power to save unbelievers. Only God does that—and we have the privilege of praying to Him on behalf of others.

As you're reading this book, I challenge you to get in your mind the names and faces of two non-believers you know. See them. Hear them. Pray for them. And then, remember with me from chapter 2 of this book what the Bible says about those folks.

I want you to see these verses again not only to remind you why the devil fights against evangelism, but also to deepen your burden for non-believers. Hear again their spiritual state:

1. **They follow the enemy**: "You used to live in sin, just like the rest of the world, obeying the devil—the commander of the powers in the unseen

world. He is the spirit at work in the hearts of those who refuse to obey God." (Ephesians 2:2)

2. **They are blinded by the god of this age**: "Satan, who is the god of this world, has blinded the minds of those who don't believe. They are unable to see the glorious light of the Good News. They don't understand this message about the glory of Christ, who is the exact likeness of God." (2 Corinthians 4:4)

3. **They live in the kingdom of darkness**. "For he has rescued us from the kingdom of darkness and transferred us into the Kingdom of his dear Son, who purchased our freedom and forgave our sins." (Colossians 1:13-14)

4. **They are caught in the devil's trap**. "Then they will come to their senses and escape from the devil's trap. For they have been held captive by him to do whatever he wants." (2 Timothy 2:26)

5. **They live in darkness under the power of Satan**. "Yes, I am sending you to the Gentiles to open their eyes, so they may turn from darkness to light and from the power of Satan to God." (Acts 26:17-18)

Do you now know why we need to pray? We're trying to reach people held under the power of Satan and his forces who want to keep them in bondage.

No evangelistic tool can fix that problem on its own.

No "testimony" by itself can convince someone to believe.

No church emphasis can free people from the devil's trap.

Even reading this book cannot make a difference by itself.

Not one of these approaches works by itself because it's only *God* who opens blinded minds, frees people from the enemy's trap, and transfers them out of darkness. *God* does it—not you and I—and He welcomes our prayers on behalf of others.

The work of evangelism must include the two things my 12-year-old friend offered to me: proclamation of the Word and the prayers of God's people. God changes hearts in response to believers telling the good news and interceding for unbelievers. In fact, I'm convinced that's why I couldn't get away from the message my buddy had told me during my seventh-grade year: he prayed even more for me during the summer break between my seventh and eighth grades. It's that simple.

Where Our Praying Should Begin

When I was a young pastor, I quickly led my little congregation in Ohio to begin praying for loved ones, friends, neighbors, and classmates who did not have a personal relationship with Jesus. I didn't have much training (I was only 20 at the time), but I did know we needed to pray. So, that's what we did.

We prayed, and then we went and told others about Jesus. We told, and then we prayed some more. Here's the way I describe our efforts in another Church Answers resource, *The Potential and Power of Prayer*.

> So productive were our evangelism efforts that we grieved as a congregation if a week passed without someone coming to Christ. How did we get there? We prayed. A lot. Together and individually. Passionately and persistently. Faithfully and fiercely. We prayed because we didn't know what else to do. And God blessed our efforts.[2]

God did indeed bless our efforts, and I thank Him annually on the day of my ministry anniversary for that sweet congregation. As I look back, though, I realize I missed one component of praying that needed more emphasis. I wouldn't change the praying we did for non-believers if I were to do it again, but I would add a prayer focus that I simply missed in my early ministry days. That is, I would have led my church to pray more for each other to be even bolder evangelists for Jesus.

Let's let the apostle Paul speak to this topic. From a prison cell, the apostle wrote these words to the believers in the area of Ephesus and Colosse, respectively:

- "And pray for me, too. Ask God to give me the right words so I can boldly explain God's mysterious plan that the Good News is for Jews and Gentiles alike. I am in chains now, still preaching

> this message as God's ambassador. So pray that I will keep on speaking boldly for him, as I should." (Ephesians 6:19-20)
- "Pray for us, too, that God will give us many opportunities to speak about his mysterious plan concerning Christ. That is why I am here in chains. Pray that I will proclaim this message as clearly as I should." (Colossians 4:3-4)

Don't miss what Paul requested. He wanted the brothers and sisters to pray that (1) he would speak boldly, (2) he would speak clearly, and (3) he would not miss opportunities to speak the message.

Boldness to speak. Clarity in message. Awareness and sensitivity to opportunities.

That's what Paul wanted others to pray for him.

What's amazing to me is not that these were Paul's requests, but that *it was Paul* making these requests in the first place. He was already in prison for speaking the gospel clearly and boldly, and now he wanted believers to pray for him to keep doing the same thing! Never did he want to stop evangelizing; never did he want to allow even prison shackles to keep him from telling the good news—so he sought intercession from the believers.

If Paul needed that kind of prayer support to evangelize, surely you and I do, too! Indeed, because we're not Paul, we need even more prayer in that direction. Can you imagine what might happen if your church's leaders began to pray that way daily for you? For other church leaders? Can you envision the evangelistic change that might occur in your congregation if you led your entire church to pray that way for each other?

Church leader, maybe this is a good starting point for you. Teach and preach the Ephesians 6 and Colossians 4 texts, and strategically and intentionally lead your church to pray accordingly. They'll begin to see people around them as sheep without a shepherd (Matt 9:36). Their hearts will begin to break over the spiritual condition of non-believers in their sphere. They will start to watch for opportunities to speak about Jesus.

Of course, this approach doesn't preclude the need to equip your church members to share the gospel. You'll still have some training to do, but that work will be less effective if your congregation isn't burdened over non-believers in the first place. It's the Word and prayer that move us into brokenness.

So, start by praying for each other to be bold, clear, and alert.

A Way to Pray for Non-Believers

Paul not only sought prayer from others, but he also showed us his own heart on behalf of unbelievers: "Dear brothers and sisters, the longing of my heart and my prayer to God is for the people of Israel to be saved" (Romans 10:1). Paul's heart burned for his people to come to know the Redeemer.

It burned so much so that he prayed for them.

As I write this chapter, I've been praying for my older sister for more than 50 years. I know prayer works, as I also prayed for my dad and mom for 36 and 47 years, respectively, before they became believers. God took longer to grab their hearts than I might have liked, but His timing was right and His grace sufficient. Both my parents passed away with the peace that only a relationship with Jesus can bring. Now, I'm praying for my sister to have the same peace in her life.

Here's the way I often pray for non-believers—and I've left blank spaces in the prayer so you might insert a name in your life. You'll quickly see that I pray using the texts listed earlier in this chapter:

> God, I pray for _____. You know he's dead in his sin. He's following the prince of the air. He's in darkness even though he doesn't know it. I don't know exactly how the enemy's keeping him blinded, but I know it's happening.
>
> God, _____ just doesn't want to listen to the gospel. He's caught in the devil's trap and living under the enemy's power.
>
> God, I can't save _____, but You can. Please, God, free _____ from his bondage. Turn his heart to the light.
>
> And, God, give me faith to believe You're somehow working in his life even though I may not see it. Amen.

May you and your church start praying evangelistically today! It's work, but it's not that complicated.

CHAPTER 7
Why Preaching is So Important

Our Church Answers team has consulted with thousands of churches. I've been privileged to do consulting for more than 25 years, and I've worked with churches of all sizes, of different denominations, and in various locations. In general, I love this work.

I don't love it, though, when I have to be honest with a pastor whose preaching is not good. I realize that judging preaching is subjective, but all of us usually know when the preaching simply isn't connecting with anyone.

It's tough to have that conversation with a pastor, but I've had to have it more than once. My general approach is to do my best to be helpful, encouraging pastors with ideas for strengthening their preaching (recognizing that I, too, still have a lot to learn about the task). Ideally, we can work together to create sermons that are biblical, practical, relevant, and engaging.

Why spend so much time helping pastors with their preaching? Because the preaching of the Word is a central way to do evangelism and to show church members how to do it.

The Fear and Weight of Preaching

To be honest, preaching itself is a bit scary to me. For example, I know I will answer to God for what I say. God will hold me accountable for every word I say, and He will not ignore any carelessness from my lips (Matt 12:36-37).

I also realize that what I do in preaching affects eternity. Here, I'm not suggesting that my preaching somehow trumps the sovereignty of God, however. I am simply aware that God uses proclamation of His Word to save souls (Rom 10:9-15) and to grow believers. That's weighty.

Further, I may have only one opportunity to speak truth to a listener. He or she may attend church only that Sunday. In the midst of a busy life, a listener may offer alert ears for only a few minutes. I will miss that one-time open door if my preaching wanders from the Word.

Then, it's also easier to talk about "stuff" than it is to really teach the Word. It's just easier to use a few Bible verses as a launching pad to preach about "stuff" than to do the hard work of Bible exposition—and that reality scares me.

Finally, I know that the devil attacks preachers. The gospel is "power of God at work, saving everyone who believes" (Rom 1:16). So, it's not unexpected the enemy aims his arrows at preachers to hinder us from preaching and living out the Word.

If you're a preacher or teacher, we encourage you to take these words to heart. You have the honor and privilege of speaking the Word of God that is "useful to teach us what is true and to make us realize what is wrong in our lives. It corrects us when we are wrong and teaches us to do what is right, [and] God uses it to prepare and equip his people to do every good work" (2 Timothy 3:16-17).

That Word is "alive and powerful. It is sharper than the sharpest two-edged sword, cutting between soul and spirit, between joint and marrow. It exposes our innermost thoughts and desires" (Hebrews 4:12).

It is the Word Jesus used to drive the devil away in His temptation in the wilderness (Matt 4:1-11).

It is the Word that gives us the gospel that "Christ died for our sins, just as the Scriptures said. He was buried, and he was raised from the dead on the third day, just as the Scriptures said" (1 Corinthians 15:3-4).

And, we get the honor and privilege of preaching that Word.

That's significant. That's heavy.

That matters, because it's the truth that sets people free (John 8:32).

And, preaching's a prime opportunity to tell the good news of Jesus.

The Work of Preaching Evangelistically

Because of my own love for preaching and evangelism, I pay attention to preachers and teachers who do a good job of using their platform to tell the gospel. Based on my own observations and conversations with many evangelistic preachers and teachers I've known, here are some of their characteristics:

They are personal evangelists themselves.

Yes, they speak the gospel from the pulpit, but that speaking is simply an overflow of their own personal walk. I can say with confidence that I have seldom met an evangelistic pulpiteer who isn't also evangelistic in his neighborhood and community.

In fact, two of my pastoral heroes whose messages always challenge me have had me in their homes, and somewhere in our conversations they've humbly and gratefully described the spiritual conditions of their neighbors. They often speak of those they've led to the Lord and of those with whom they're still working. It is as if these faithful brothers almost can't help but talk about their personal burden for those who live around them. Knowing that, I realize even more why evangelism comes through in their preaching and teaching.

They pray fervently for non-believers around them.

Again, I'm speaking of men I know well enough to have heard their prayers and to have learned how to pray from them. They understand the spiritual condition of non-believers we described earlier in this book, and they know only God can open blinded minds and free trapped people.

So, they pray.

Uncessingly.

By name for non-believers.

Their hearts are so burdened by lostness that their conversations with God quickly go there. Their sermons then reflect that same burden.

They recognize their pulpit opportunities in emphasizing evangelism.

With a focus I'll discuss again below, they preach the Word with a decided focus on Jesus. They know the Word is God's message of redemption, and they want their neighbors and the nations to know that story. At the same time, they illustrate evangelism in their sermons, celebrate conversion stories in their messages, and emphasize churchwide evangelism as needed in their announcements. These preachers know others listen to their voice, so they use the platform God has given them to push the Great Commission responsibility to make disciples.

They intentionally point to Jesus in their messages.

Evangelistic preachers and teachers I known simply teach the Word, showing that all of it ultimately points to Jesus—as He Himself said to His disciples on the road to Emmaus: "'Wasn't it clearly predicted that the Messiah would have to suffer all these things before entering his glory?' Then Jesus took them through the writings of Moses and all the prophets, explaining from all the Scriptures the things concerning himself" (Luke 24:26-27).

The preachers I'm describing here don't miss the opportunity to speak about the Redeemer in their messages. And, they make sure their listeners know that Jesus is the only way to the Father (John 14:6).

They're unafraid to share with their church their evangelistic burdens and actions.

They don't "pat themselves on the back" for their evangelism, but nor do they shy away from telling their own experiences in their preaching. Imagine how a congregation might hear these words from their pastor when he uses them appropriately during a sermon:

> "I've been trying to share the gospel with a neighbor in my community who just doesn't want to listen. Would you join me in praying for him when you pray?"

> "This past week, my wife and I spent time with a friend we've been seeking to lead to the Lord. She asked us this important question that I want to answer from the Word today: 'I think there are multiple ways to God as long as you're a good person. What do you think about that?'"

> "Each week, I spend one afternoon in the downtown square getting to know people in our

community. I want to know them so I might get an opportunity to help them know Jesus."

"Like some of you, I've been praying for a wayward adult son for many years now. I so much want him to follow Jesus, and I struggle sometimes with God's apparent delay in responding to my prayer—but still I trust Him."

See, a sermon is a great opportunity to remind believers of the need to evangelize, to describe for them what an evangelistic life looks like, and to invite them to join you in prayer for non-believers. Where appropriate when teaching or preaching the Word, illustrate biblical truths with your own evangelistic efforts. Do it humbly, but do it.

They work hard to "draw the net" in their sermons.

Your church might call the time an "invitation" or "response time," but it's a time when preachers challenge their listeners to respond rightly to the preached Word. These evangelistic pastors clearly and concisely tell their congregation how to follow Christ by turning from sin and trusting Him with their lives.

Their efforts to call people to Christ are intentional, passionate, and genuine. And, they do it almost every week. Even if any non-believers in the congregation choose not to obey Christ that day, they will know what they need to do should they choose to follow Christ later in the week. That's because the preacher intentionally made it clear the preceding Sunday.

A Challenge to Preachers

Some years ago, I made a trip to a part of the world where the believers had only portions of the Bible in their language. They devoured what they had, and they deeply longed for more. Here's how I described what happened next in a Church Answers blog post I wrote:

> I came back to the States after that trip, and I began to notice *just how many copies of the Bible I have* in my house. Like many of us, I suspect, I have far more Bibles in my house than we have human beings. I have the entirety of God's Word in my language and in my hands, and I can open any copy freely without threat to my life. I'm privileged to have God's Word, to be able to read God's Word, and to proclaim God's Word. I continue these days to realize just how blessed I am—quite undeservedly so—to be a child of God who called me to Himself and who speaks to me through His Word.[3]

And, as I think about closing this chapter, I'm amazed that God allows me to preach His Word at all. For whatever reason, He has trusted me and so many others to be His voice, His spokesperson, His witness to a world in need of a Savior. Sunday after Sunday, I get to tell

WHY PREACHING IS SO IMPORTANT

the good news to people whose lives are often filled with not-so-good news.

I truly don't understand why God any of us do this work. . . . except that He's grace. He's mercy. He's good.

He's worth talking about.

He's worth talking about not only on Sunday, but on Monday, Tuesday, Wednesday, Thursday, Friday, and Saturday, too.

We might preach on Sunday most of the time, but we can talk about Jesus every day. We can do evangelism daily even as we prepare to evangelize from the pulpit.

And, when we lead the way to do evangelism—beginning with our preaching—our church will become evangelistic.

Hear us again—it's not rocket science.

CHAPTER 8
The Evangelistic Small Group

In our Church Answers consulting work and in my personal consulting work prior to joining Church Answers, we have sent "secret shoppers" to churches to get their first impressions of the church's on-campus small groups (if they have them) and the church's worship services.

We could tell you all kinds of stories of what our secret shoppers have experienced, but let me give you just a few reports of their experiences in small groups:

- "I got there on time—at the time the group was to start. Actually, I was the only one there for the first ten minutes."
- "About 15 people came in the room, and no one spoke to me until the teacher came in and said, 'Hi.'"
- "The teaching was good. It was all lecture, which is not my preference, but it was good."
- "They told me this class would be friendly, but I didn't find it that way. They seemed friendly to each other, but not to me."
- "I enjoyed the class, but no one showed us where to go after the class ended. We had to find our way

to where our kids were in their own class, and then we just followed the crowd to the worship center."
- "Several people greeted us before the class started. The teaching and the interaction were really good. I would go back to this group if I visited again."

Needless to say, the last report is an unusual one. What our shoppers usually find is evidence that the group is inwardly focused and hardly expecting guests to attend.

To be fair, we realize that some small groups are closed groups designed for short-term study or life-on-life discipleship among believers. We're not talking about these types of groups in this chapter. What we're talking about are small groups the church *wants* to be outwardly-focused; We're talking about small groups who *should* be evangelistic.

These are typically the types of groups our Church Answers secret shoppers have attended. They're supposed to be outposts of gospel witness who welcome guests and non-believers, but our shoppers checking out the group sometimes feel almost like unwelcome intruders in a family meeting.

That kind of group is hardly likely to be evangelistic.

A Different Picture

Compare that first story to this description of a small group in the second church I pastored in Ohio. Their leader was an excellent teacher/facilitator. Their group loved fellowshipping. They shared life together, bearing each others' burdens and celebrating each family's victories. It really was a great group that church members often talked about.

That group was different from other groups, though. They were intentionally evangelistic.

Every week, they talked about family and friends they wanted to reach for Christ. Every week, they prayed for non-believers by name. Twice a year, they scheduled events with the goal of inviting unchurched people to come and see it can be fun to be with church people. The members almost automatically greeted guests when they showed up on Sunday. Because their teacher briefly shared the plan of salvation each week, the class members also knew their guests who came would hear the gospel. Without exception.

And, this group multiplied itself almost every year. In fact—and I realize these words might sound like hyperbole—this group was so committed to multiplying that they grieved a bit when they didn't. They rejoiced and celebrated when group members got saved, and they walked with new believers to get them started on their journey. Then, they sent out their best to start another group who would join the first group in reaching their community. Two strong groups with evangelism in their DNA always set the example for other groups in our church.

These groups modeled what our Church Answers friend Kevin Mills wrote in his book, *How to Lead a Healthy Small Group*:

> Healthy small groups may be the best and most effective evangelism tool for your church. Every person on the planet needs healthy, dynamic relationships. . . . the vast majority of people in the world desperately need and eagerly desire close connections with others. Therefore, a healthy, thriving small group ministry will attract the lost and the lonely to your church and to the gospel.[4]

And, I might add in light of the topic of this book, a healthy, thriving small group ministry will compel group members to go tell others about what God's doing through the group. That's the way it's supposed to work.

It's really that simple. Your church's small groups can be evangelistic.

Your church's small groups *should* be evangelistic.

What Happens Too Often

I wish I could say that every group in our church followed the example I just described, but that's not the case. Even the groups that started with the strongest outward focus often turned inwardly at some point. Few groups I know want to be inwardly focused, but it happens. Often.

Here are some reasons why it does.

Their churches are already inwardly focused.
It's not just the Sunday school class or small group that looks inwardly—it's the whole church. In those settings,

classes and groups almost inevitably turn inwardly focused.

Many class and group members have never been discipled to be Great Commission-focused.

In fact, they've frequently not been discipled at all. That failure often means that they still focus more on self than on others.

Internal fellowship becomes more important than the mission.

That's not to deny the significance of fellowship; it's simply to say that it's tough to maintain an outward focus as the group gels and loves being together.

The church chooses teachers and facilitators who aren't themselves outwardly focused.

And, it's not that they don't see the need to be outwardly-focused; it's just that they don't naturally lean in that direction. Eventually, the spirit and passion of the leader influence the group in the wrong direction.

The group develops such "life-on-life" accountability that they don't want anyone else in the group.

On one hand, this level of spiritual intimacy is a good thing. On the other hand, though, it can close the door to outreach. Perhaps groups need to work more at learning to do both outreach and accountability, with the latter likely taking place in an even smaller group at a different time.

They run out of room.
When the group meeting space reaches capacity, it's often the case that the group loses its outward focus and stops growing. That almost naturally happens when there's no more room for more people.

The teacher or facilitator gets comfortable with his or her "own" group.
We don't know many Sunday school teachers or small group leaders who start out thinking this way, but it sometimes occurs when the group reaches a point of consistency and depth. Leaders work hard to hang on to the group members they have, and they think less about reaching others.

The group's not thinking about multiplication.
Reproducing themselves by sending out group members to plant new Sunday school classes or small groups isn't even in their view. Who wants to grow something and then give up the growth you've worked so hard to achieve?

Do any of these reasons characterize your church? Your small group? If so, we again have good news for you: your group(s) can become evangelistic again. Let's talk about how that might happen.

Turning a Small Group Outward: Leading Them to Do Evangelism

We might surprise you (and perhaps bother you, if you're a group leader) with our first suggestion for turning a small group outward, but we're convinced it's right based on years of studying congregations: if you want your small groups to be evangelistic, you have to enlist small group leaders who are themselves already evangelistic.

Just like we've said throughout this book about churches in general, small groups aren't evangelistic because their leaders aren't evangelistic.

Sure, even the most evangelistic group leader probably won't convince everyone in the group to be evangelistic, but it's fairly certain that a non-evangelistic group leader won't convince anyone. That's a problem if you want your church to be evangelistic.

Hear us, though. We're not at all suggesting you should recruit group leaders who are evangelistic but have no giftedness in facilitating or teaching a small group. We're not calling for evangelism at the expense of excellent teaching of the Word. What we're suggesting is that you need to enlist potential group leaders who do both well.

Already we can hear the voices of our readers, though: "We can't find group leaders anyway. And, our church doesn't do much evangelism. How in the world can we do what you're saying?" We get the question, and we'd probably ask the same question about many churches we've studied. We do think there's a solution, however. . . .

Start with only one or two groups at a time.

Don't worry upfront about getting every small group to be evangelistic. Focus on just a couple groups whose leaders at least seem to think outwardly, and work with them. Help the leader to maximize his or her evangelistic efforts. If necessary, enlist a co-leader whose heart beats with evangelism, and trust his spirit will influence the other leader toward doing the Great Commission even more.

Train those groups to share their testimonies with each other, like the church we described in chapter 1 of this book. Challenge them to lead the way for the church by sharing their stories with unchurched folks and inviting them to church. With their permission, use their stories as sermon illustrations and announcement reinforcements. You might be surprised by the powerful influence of a few small groups whose embers of evangelism soon spread to other groups in the congregation.

Just one or two small group leaders.

Just one or two groups.

It doesn't take much to light a fire for evangelism in your church.

Simple Ways to Get It Done

Assume with us that you have some group leaders who are evangelistic and who are already influencing group members toward doing evangelism. Here are some simple strategies, then, to keep a small group turned in the right direction:

1. **Every time the group gathers, pray for (1) the members to share the gospel boldly and for (2) God to melt the hearts of non-believers and free them from the devil's trap.** Praying for members and non-believers *by name* only raises the significance of the prayer for everyone in the room.
2. **Ask one member each week to share his or her testimony of God's grace.** You've heard this idea before, of course. Help group members see that all of us are trophies of God's grace, and they'll be more excited to tell others about Jesus. And, they'll have a model each week showing them how to do it.
3. **Within the group, develop prayer partners who pray Ephesians 6:18-20 and Colossians 4:2-4 for each other.** Maybe you remember that we talked about those verses in chapter 6 of this book. Now, we're suggesting again that you follow the biblical texts in praying for boldness, clarity, and opportunity.
4. **Trust that God will work through your efforts.**

It's really that simple. It's obedience and trust.

CHAPTER 9
Our Great Omission: Why Evangelistic Churches are Evangelistic

For almost forty years, our team at Church Answers has been researching and studying churches, primarily those in North America. Several of us have had the joy of serving as lead pastor of churches God blessed with evangelistic growth. We've written books about the church in America. Our team's passion has been leading and learning about evangelistic churches. Still, we have not given sufficient attention to one of the primary characteristics of evangelistic churches.

Our Great Omission

It is so obvious. Indeed, it is so clear that we are surprised at our neglect of this factor. Stated simply, here's the factor: *the evangelistic churches that we have researched for the past forty years have one or more highly evangelistic Christians.*

We know the previous statement is no great revelation. It surely is stating the obvious. But, if it is reality, why have we not written more about these Christians who have a passion for evangelism? Why are we not doing a better job of telling their stories even now?

Why are we spending so much time discussing church models, worship styles, digital strategies, or discipleship curricula, and not enough time focusing on the individual Christians God is using to bring people to Christ?

In this chapter, we will address this great omission by shining a light on what God is already doing through His people. It's time we celebrate these stories. It's time we amplify them. And, it's time we ask what we might learn from them.

The Real Difference-Makers

When you walk into an evangelistic church, you will often find certain visible markers: a welcoming atmosphere, clear preaching of the gospel, and mission-minded leadership. But beneath all those elements, there is often something else—or, more specifically, *someone* else.

Someone whose name you may not know.

A person who isn't always on the platform.

Just a quiet but persistent voice for Christ in the workplace, at the gym, in the school pickup line, or across the kitchen table.

The real difference-makers in evangelistic churches are not always the ones with a title. They are the ones with a burden—the ones who carry gospel conversations in their hearts as seriously as most people carry their calendars on their phones, the ones who cannot imagine a week going by without praying for a lost person by name.

We've spoken with dozens of pastors who have said something like this to our team: "We started seeing more people come to Christ, and when we traced it back, it always led to the same person." It could be a schoolteacher. A retired grandmother. A college student. Or anyone genuinely in love with Jesus. But, what they had in common was a contagious faith and a consistent pattern of gospel conversations.

Seven Characteristics of Highly Evangelistic Christians

It is inevitable that, when we do research on evangelistic churches, we learn about one or more members in the church who, to use the book title by Charles H. Spurgeon, embody the traits of *The Soul Winner*. One of those members is often the pastor, but we have also seen many laypersons who are themselves soul winners.

In our interviews with these people, or with those who tell us about the soul winners, we began to discern some clear patterns. Our team has called those patterns "the seven characteristics of highly evangelistic Christians." Let's walk through each of them.

1. They are people of prayer.

There is no shortcut here. Evangelistic Christians spend time with God before they spend time talking about God. They realize that only God can convict and convert, and they are totally dependent upon Him in prayer. Some of the highly evangelistic Christians we've studied spend as much as an hour in prayer each day—not out of obligation, but out of desperation. They pray for specific people by name. They pray for divine appointments. And, they pray for boldness when the moment arrives.

2. They have a theology that compels them to evangelize.

Their motivation is not merely emotional or circumstantial. It is rooted in what they believe about God, sin, salvation, and eternity. They believe in the urgency of the gospel message. They believe that Christ is the only way of salvation. They believe that anyone without Christ is doomed for a literal hell. That's not a popular view in many circles today, but it is the fuel behind their fervency. Right theology leads to right passion.

3. They spend time in the Word.

The more time they spend in the Bible, the more likely they are to see the lostness of humanity and the love of God in Christ to save those who are lost. The Word of God not only informs their minds; it ignites their hearts. Some of the evangelistic Christians we've encountered have a Bible that is worn, marked, and often tear-stained. They see the gospel not as good advice, but as the central truth of Scripture.

4. They are compassionate people.

Their hearts break for those who don't have a personal relationship with Jesus Christ. They have learned to love the world by becoming more like Christ who has the greatest love for the world. Their evangelism is not driven by duty, but by compassion. They don't see "projects"; they see people with names, stories, and eternal destinies. They ache for the prodigals, the skeptics, the broken, and the blind to come to Jesus.

5. They love the communities where God has placed them.

They are evangelistic where they live because they believe God has sovereignly placed them there. They are immersed in the culture because they desire for the light of Christ to shine through them in their communities. They coach Little League. They attend city council meetings. They are the neighbors everyone knows. They're not trying to be "relevant"—they're trying to be present.

6. They are intentional about evangelism.

They pray for opportunities to share the gospel. They look for those opportunities. And, they see many so-called casual encounters as appointments God has set for them. They are not pushy, but they are purposeful. They are always planting seeds, and sometimes they get to reap the harvest. Evangelism is not something they "do" once a month—it is something they are always ready to do.

7. They are accountable to someone for their evangelistic activities.

They know that many good activities can replace Great Commission activities if they are not careful. Good can replace the best, so they make certain that someone holds them accountable, either formally or informally, for their evangelistic efforts. Some have prayer partners who do it. Some are part of small groups that ask hard questions. They welcome accountability that keeps evangelism from becoming an afterthought.

Imagine what would happen if every church had just five people with these characteristics. Or even three people. Or even one person. Or, imagine what might happen if others had at least a few of these seven characteristics. Whether it's just a few people with a few of these characteristics, or at least five people with all the characteristics, things will not stay the same. The gospel would begin to echo down every hallway, through every neighborhood, and into every hurting home.

The "Secret" of Evangelistic Churches

The secret is really no secret at all. Ultimately, evangelistic churches see more persons become Christians because of the passionate efforts of highly evangelistic Christians.

You've heard us say it before in this book, but it bears repeating again: *these churches become evangelistic churches because their church members do evangelism.* People are still the instruments God has chosen to use.

Yes, churches need structure. They need clarity. They need resources and strategies. But, none of those can replace the faithful witness of a Spirit-empowered Christian who says, "Let me tell you what Jesus has done in my life."

The "secret" of evangelistic churches is believer after believer, who, like the unnamed woman at the well in John 4, announce to their city, "Come and see a man!" (John 4:29). It's the believer who, like the unidentified person who directed the blood-diseased woman to Jesus in Mark 5:27, isn't worried about whether his or her name shows up in the story. It's believers like my 12-year-old classmate who kept telling me about Jesus not because he wanted teenage recognition, but simply because he loved God and me.

It's you and I when our passion for Jesus is so great we almost can't help but talk about Jesus.

The "secret" of evangelistic churches is evangelistic people who have no desire to keep Jesus a secret from purposeless neighbors and hurting peoples around the world.

An Encouraging Trend

Let us offer a word of encouragement. We are seeing more pastors intentionally identifying and developing soul winners in their congregations. These pastors are not merely asking for volunteers to fill roles—they are praying for God to raise up evangelistic champions in the spirit of Luke 10:2. And when they find champions, they don't let them operate in isolation. They ask these evangelistic believers to mentor others, to share stories, and to become a "living curriculum" for the church.

As we continue to study and consult with churches, we are committing to tell more of these stories, like the widow who shares Christ at her senior center, the businessman who leads a Bible study before the office opens, the college student who welcomes questions about Christianity from skeptics, or the teenager who invites friends to youth group week after week.

If we want our churches to be more evangelistic, we must lift up these models—not to exalt them, but to encourage the body of Christ. God is still using ordinary believers to do extraordinary work. We cannot miss the opportunity this time to tell these stories.

A Challenge

Charles Spurgeon was right. We need soul winners. In fact, here's the way he put it:

> "Soul-winning is the chief business of the Christian minister; indeed, it should be the main pursuit of every true believer. We should each say with Simon Peter, 'I go a fishing,' and with Paul our aim should be, 'That I might by all means save some.'"[5]

Later in his book, he would add this penetrating point: "Do you above all things aim at saving souls? I am afraid that some have forgotten this grand object but, dear friends, anything short of this is unworthy to be the great end of a Christian's life."[6]

We need soul winners, but they will not come from a conference. They will not emerge from a campaign. They will arise when Christians, often ordinary and overlooked, get on their knees in prayer, open the Word of God, see the brokenness around them, and move toward the lost with gospel hope.

The great omission that precipitated the writing of this chapter is only an omission if we let it remain hidden.

Let's not let it.

Let's shine a light on the soul winners in our midst.

Let's pray for more of them.

And, by God's grace, let's become one of them.

CHAPTER 10
A Discipleship Pathway that Leads to Evangelism

Let me take you back to where this book began by telling you a story.

I wish you could see what hangs in a stairway in our house. You probably can't read it, as it's written in Chinese. I can't read it, either, to be honest, but I do know what it says:

> Jesus came and told his disciples, "I have been given all authority in heaven and on earth. Therefore, go and make disciples of all the nations, baptizing them in the name of the Father and the Son and the Holy Spirit. Teach these new disciples to obey all the commands I have given you. And be sure of this: I am with you always, even to the end of the age." (Matt 28:18-20)

You likely recognize Matthew's account of the Great Commission. This banner, a gift from a former student whose Chinese father-in-law hand prepared it for me, reminds me that believers all around the world have this mandate from our Lord. No matter where we live, God expects us to make disciples—so let's talk about that mandate again.

"Make Disciples"—What Does It Mean?

Too often, we've heard believers limit this concept of making disciples to what we might commonly call "discipleship" today—that is, it's about teaching believers to be better believers. That's certainly one part of this mandate, but it's hardly the full extent of the commission Jesus gave us.

Instead, making disciples begins the very moment when we challenge someone to turn to Christ and *become* His disciple. The process starts not when a non-believer has just become a Christian, but when a believer first tells the good news to that non-believer. It's when someone like the passionate believers in the previous chapter says to an unbeliever, "I'd love to talk to you about what it means to be a follower of Jesus."

When that non-believer follows Christ, the disciplemaking process continues with baptism in the name of the Father, the Son, and the Holy Spirit—a public marker that a new believer has new life in the resurrected Christ. I can still remember with deep appreciation the day my pastor (whose title I didn't yet understand) baptized me as a 13-year-old. Maybe you remember that day in your life, too.

Still, the work of disciplemaking isn't over with the baptism, either. Jesus was clear that our task next is to teach new believers to obey all the commands He has given us. Those commands, by the way, include the very command—the Great Commission—we're looking at right now. That means we disciple new believers who obey Jesus by making disciples themselves who also obey Jesus.

That also means this process doesn't end. Disciples make disciples who make disciples who make disciples. From the first believer telling the good news to a non-believer, the journey keeps going as new believers become evangelistic themselves so others might follow Jesus, too. Disciplers do teach disciples to obey everything that Jesus commanded, but teaching them to tell the good news themselves is critical to the Great Commission.

But, Something Happens

I wish I could say that every new believer catches fire for Jesus, evangelizes family and friends, and teaches other believers to walk well with Jesus, but that doesn't always happen. Too often, their fire dies down. Their zeal disappears. Their evangelism stops. In fact, I fear we've come to expect this process with most new believers.

What happens to the fire? I could list several causes, but here's the primary one: *churches have too little (if anything) already in place to keep fueling the fire.*

They reach non-believers, baptize them, and then expect them to figure out the rest of their journey on their own. The church may have the components of good discipleship in place (though many churches aren't even that strong), but nobody helps the baby believer know how to navigate them.

The result? The enemy we described in chapter 2 of this book aims his arrows at new believers who are fighting alone a battle they don't even recognize—and that zealous, passionate follower of Jesus becomes a routine, settled down, defeated church member.

And, we might add in light of this book, he or she becomes a *non-evangelistic* church member.

To use an image that most of us will understand, that's what happens when the church doesn't have the discipleship nursery ready for the new life that God brings their way.

We don't want that to happen when your church becomes an evangelistic church.

So, What Do We Do?

We can't in a single chapter resolve this issue, but we can give you some steps to move in the right direction. Based on our interactions with churches over the years who've worked hard to address this issue, here are some of those steps.

Enlist a discipleship/equipping prayer team.

Don't try to address this problem on your own. Enlist some prayer warriors who will join you in asking God to give wisdom to you and your church's leaders. And, we recommend that this prayer team become a standing prayer team since the process of disciplemaking doesn't end.

Church leader, begin investing in another believer now.

Your church's discipleship work can be stronger *today* if you start investing in a younger believer or even in an older believer who's never been discipled. You'll still need to work on developing a churchwide discipleship pathway, but start by inviting another believer to lunch. Have a conversation. See where the Lord takes it. Like everything else in this book, it doesn't have to be complicated.

Work with your church's leaders to define and describe a biblical "disciple" for your congregation.

If your church can't describe with biblical clarity what you expect a disciple of Christ to be, know, believe, and do, you're likely going through the motions of discipleship without direction. As I've written in another Church Answers resource, all the discipleship puzzle pieces may be there, but they're all lying on the floor because nobody knows what the puzzle's supposed to look like in the first place.[7] The problem is that an undefined discipleship target quickly becomes an undiscipled disciple.

Think discipleship pathway in terms of corporate worship, small groups, and mentoring.[8]

All three components should contribute to your church's process of growing the biblical disciples you intend to grow. Preach with intentionality. Plan small group curriculum and emphases with intentionality. Invest in others with intentionality. Strive so that everything you do leads to non-believers becoming believers who then reproduce themselves in other believers, too. All along the way, we also encourage you to look at our Church Equip curriculum to help you.

Emphasize small groups, beginning with a membership class.

I've never known a disciple-making church without a strong, intentional small group ministry that promotes life-on-life Christian growth. Accountability, training, and encouragement mark these groups. So, prayerfully enlist the best small group leaders you can find. Equip them well. Hold them accountable. At the same time, put in place a membership class (preferably, a required one) that is much more than a content-based, vision-casting entrance into the church; make it the place where church leaders explain what they expect of new members and describe how they will help members be committed Christ-followers. Let it be a first step in the church's discipleship pathway.

Challenge new believers to begin evangelizing as soon as they become believers.

My pastor told me quickly to start telling others what Jesus meant to me when God saved me, and I did just what he said. I hadn't received any training yet. I didn't have answers to all my questions. Writing books on evangelism was hardly on my radar. What I did have, though, was a story—a story like those we've pointed to throughout this book. I was only a 13-year-old rookie believer, but I could tell others, "Hey, I've learned that Jesus loves me so much that He died for me." My church wasn't the best at making disciples, but they were wise enough to tell me to do evangelism when my fire was hottest and my access to non-believers was closest.

Build evangelism and discipleship evaluation into your church's system.

If you believe this work matters—and it does—evaluate it. Annually ask questions like:

- What percentage of our members regularly attend a worship service? are involved in a small group? are in a mentoring relationship?
- What percentage have been trained to tell their gospel story?
- What percentage can tell the gospel clearly?
- What percentage can name at least five non-believers who are genuine friends, and for whom they're praying?

- What percentage have evangelized someone within the last three months? Six months? A year?
- What percentage of our church's growth in the last year has come from conversions rather than transfer growth?
- Are we satisfied with all of these findings? If not, what steps will we take to address any that need attention?

In some ways, this last question may be the most important one. If you work through this list, recognize areas of needed improvement, and then only talk about suggestions, you won't have gone very far. You might feel better because you've asked the right questions, but it's doubtful your church will be more Great Commission-oriented. It's even more dubious that your congregation will be more Great Commission-obedient.

If you don't start somewhere with an action step, you also won't get anywhere. So, let's do this: take some time right now to ask the Lord, "What's the first step I need to take to lead my church to become an evangelistic church?" Then, write your answer somewhere where you can keep it in front of you continually.

Pray about it on the go.

Share it with another church leader who will join you in praying and doing.

Then, do it. Take the first step. Get started.

It's really that simple.

A Final Challenge

We assume you picked up this book because you want your church to be an evangelistic church. That can happen, as we hope you believe as you work toward the end of this study.

It might be, however, that you—even though you're likely a church leader—have never been discipled well, nor do you have the evangelistic fire you once had. You come to the end of this book with some ideas for your congregation, but you also come to this conclusion with some conviction over your own heart.

You recognize that any change in your church's evangelistic focus has to start with you. If that's where you are, first know that our Church Answers team has made a commitment to pray regularly for anyone reading this book. We understand your struggles because we sometimes walk in your shoes.

Second, invite another believer to help you grow in Christ and strengthen your evangelistic passion. Try to make changes on your own, and the enemy will come after you in your isolation. Lean on others, and together watch what God does in moving the heart of your congregation to evangelism.

We'll say it one more time: it's really not that complicated.

Conclusion

Our Church Answers team thanks you for joining us on this journey. We wish we could walk with each of you personally to see what the Lord is going to do in your life, but we realize we may never meet this side of eternity. We do trust, though, that we will someday together see the evangelistic fruit of your life and the lives of your congregation.

In the meantime, we ask you to say a prayer for us, too. We don't want to be only writing and teaching about evangelism.

We want to be doing it.

We *must* be doing it.

We *must* be modeling it.

We *must* be praying, going, and telling.

It's really that simple for us, too.

Endnotes

[1] Thom S. Rainer, *Effective Evangelistic Churches*. Kindle Edition, loc. 481-511.

[2] Chuck Lawless, *The Potential and Power of Prayer: How to Unleash the Praying Church* (Church Answers Resources) (p. 2). Kindle Edition.

[3] https://churchanswers.com/blog/a-surprising-first-step-pastors-toward-strengthening-your-evangelism/

[4] Kevin Mills, *How to Lead a Healthy Small Group: A Practical and Easy-to-Use Guide* (Church Answers Resources) (p. 21-22). Kindle Edition.

[5] Charles H. Spurgeon, *The Soul-Winner: or How to Lead Sinners to the Saviour* (p. 2). Kindle Edition.

[6] Ibid., p. 155.

[7] Chuck Lawless, *Disciple: How to Create a Community That Develops Passionate and Healthy Followers of Jesus* (Church Answers Resources) (p. 5). Kindle Edition.

[8] Ibid., p. 84.

www.ingramcontent.com/pod-product-compliance
Lightning Source LLC
Chambersburg PA
CBHW060202050426
42446CB00013B/2962